ATLANTIC OCEAN

N

Distance

D1309877

New York

LONG ISLAND

Newark

Trenton

Delaware

N.J.

95

Philadelphia

Harrisburg

Dover

Annapolis DEL.

Washington, D.C.

MD.

Baltimore

Chesapeake Bay

Susquehanna

80

Potomac

95

Bridge at Harpers Ferry

Shenandoah National Park

64

Richmond

95

85

95

40

81

James

VIRGINIA

Winston-Salem

Raleigh

NORTH CAROLINA

WEST VIRGINIA

64

Charleston

Mt. Rogers National Recreation Area

77

SOUTH CAROLINA

Columbia

Ohio

77

KENTUCKY

81

Little Tennessee River

20

TENNESSEE

Great Smoky Mountains National Park

Tennessee

Savannah

Springer Mtn.

85

GEORGIA

Little

CAROL M. HIGHSMITH AND TED LANDPHAIR

APPALACHIAN TRAIL

A PHOTOGRAPHIC TOUR

CRESCENT BOOKS

NEW YORK

This 1999 edition is published by Crescent Books®,
a division of Random House Value Publishing, Inc.,
201 East 50th Street, New York, N.Y. 10022.

Crescent Books and colophon are trademarks of
Random House Value Publishing, Inc.

Random House
New York • Toronto • London • Sydney • Auckland
http://www.randomhouse.com/

Printed and bound in China

Library of Congress Cataloging-in-Publication
Data
Highsmith, Carol M., 1946–
Appalachian Trail /
Carol M. Highsmith and Ted Landphair.
p.   cm. — (A photographic tour)
Includes index.
ISBN 0-517-20400-2 (hc: alk. paper)
1. Appalachian Trail—Pictorial works.
2. Appalachian Trail—Tours. I. Landphair, Ted,
1942-   . II. Title. III. Series: Highsmith,
Carol M., 1946–   Photographic tour.
F106.H47 1999   98–35690
917.404´43—dc21   CIP

8   7   6   5   4   3   2

Project Editor: Donna Lee Lurker
Production Supervisor: Milton Wackerow
Designed by Robert L. Wiser, Archetype Press, Inc.,
Washington, D.C.

All photographs by Carol M. Highsmith
unless otherwise credited: map by XNR
Productions, page 5; quilt by Mary Sands,
Louisville, Kentucky, page 6; Appalachian Trail
Conference, pages 8–15, 17–21; Inn at Long Trail,
Killington, Vermont, page 16.

THE AUTHORS ALSO WISH TO THANK
THE FOLLOWING FOR THEIR GENEROUS
ASSISTANCE AND HOSPITALITY
IN CONNECTION WITH THE COMPLETION
OF THIS BOOK

Appalachian Trail Conference,
Harpers Ferry, West Virginia
Brian King, Director of Public Affairs

Comfort Suites, Salem, Virginia

Country Inn & Suites, Roanoke, Virginia

Destinnations New England, Reservations and
Itineraries, West Yarmouth, Massachusetts

Fontana Village Resort, Fontana, North Carolina

Inn at Mills Falls, Meredith, New Hampshire

Mount Washington Hotel & Resort,
Bretton Woods, New Hampshire

Nancy Marshall Communications
on behalf of Maine Office of Tourism

New England Outdoor Center/ Twin Pine Camps,
Millinocket, Maine

Peachgove Inn, Warwick, New York
John and Lucy Mastropierro, Innkeepers

Rockfish Gap Outfitters, Waynesboro, Virginia

Lynne Liscek Black, Coastal Fairfield County
Convention and Visitor Bureau

Lars Botzojorns, Green Mountain Club
Waterbury Center, Vermont

Susan Cayea, Orange County, New York,
Director of Tourism, Goshen, New York

Don Cogswell, Appalachian Trail Cafe
Millinocket, Maine

Oren Coin, Smoky Mountain Host,
Franklin, North Carolina

Catherine Fox,
Roanoke Convention & Visitors Bureau

Jane Greber, Susquehanna Appalachian
Trail Club, Mechanicsburg, Pennsylvania

David Hooke, Dartmouth Outing Club
Hanover, New Hampshire

Fran Leckie, Old Dominion Appalachian
Trail Club, Richmond, Virginia

Karen Leggett-Abouraya, Alpharetta, Georgia

John Neff, Maine Appalachian Trail Club
Winthrop, Maine

Doug Nelson, Old Dominion Appalachian Trail
Club, Fort Lee, Virginia

Patricia O'Dell, York Hiking Club
Fawn Grove, Pennsylvania

Carol Pearson, Voice of America,
Washington, D.C.

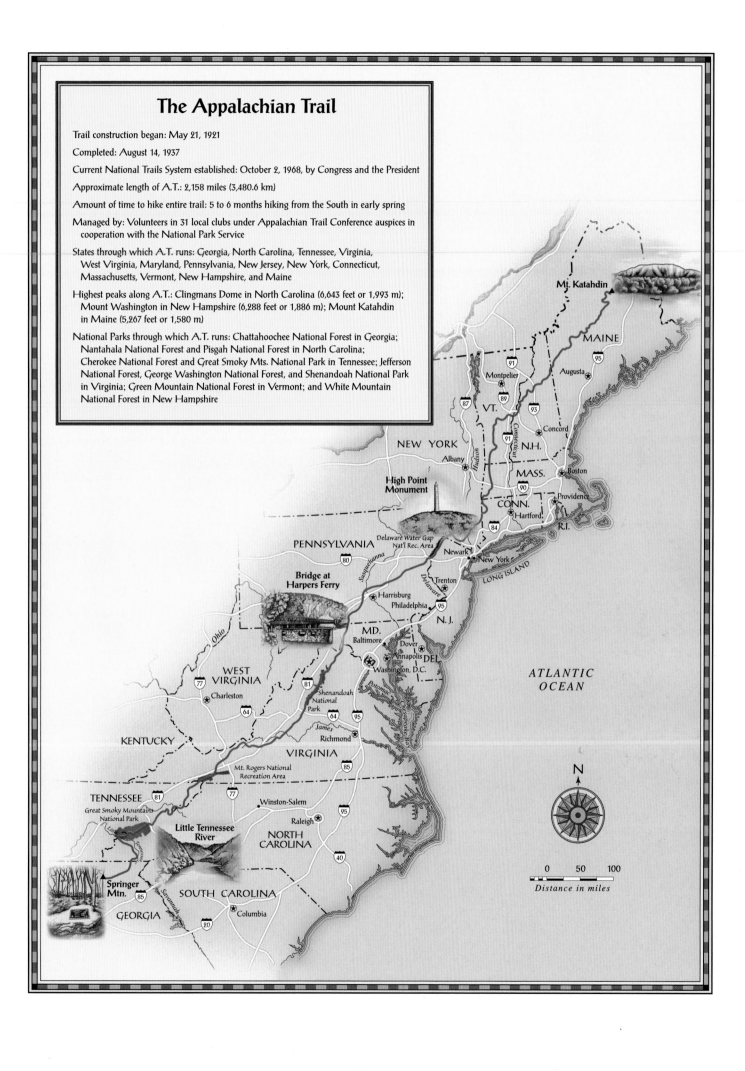

The Appalachian Trail

Trail construction began: May 21, 1921

Completed: August 14, 1937

Current National Trails System established: October 2, 1968, by Congress and the President

Approximate length of A.T.: 2,158 miles (3,480.6 km)

Amount of time to hike entire trail: 5 to 6 months hiking from the South in early spring

Managed by: Volunteers in 31 local clubs under Appalachian Trail Conference auspices in cooperation with the National Park Service

States through which A.T. runs: Georgia, North Carolina, Tennessee, Virginia, West Virginia, Maryland, Pennsylvania, New Jersey, New York, Connecticut, Massachusetts, Vermont, New Hampshire, and Maine

Highest peaks along A.T.: Clingmans Dome in North Carolina (6,643 feet or 1,993 m); Mount Washington in New Hampshire (6,288 feet or 1,886 m); Mount Katahdin in Maine (5,267 feet or 1,580 m)

National Parks through which A.T. runs: Chattahoochee National Forest in Georgia; Nantahala National Forest and Pisgah National Forest in North Carolina; Cherokee National Forest and Great Smoky Mts. National Park in Tennessee; Jefferson National Forest, George Washington National Forest, and Shenandoah National Park in Virginia; Green Mountain National Forest in Vermont; and White Mountain National Forest in New Hampshire

Mt. Katahdin

MAINE

Montpelier

Augusta

VT.

Concord

NEW YORK

N.H.

Albany

MASS.

Boston

High Point
Monument

CONN.

Providence

Hartford

R.I.

PENNSYLVANIA

Delaware Water Gap
Nat'l Rec. Area

Newark

New York

LONG ISLAND

Bridge at
Harpers Ferry

Susquehanna

Trenton

Harrisburg

Philadelphia

N.J.

Ohio

MD.

Baltimore

Dover

Annapolis

DEL.

Washington, D.C.

WEST
VIRGINIA

Charleston

Shenandoah
National
Park

ATLANTIC
OCEAN

Potomac

Chesapeake Bay

KENTUCKY

James

Richmond

VIRGINIA

Mt. Rogers National
Recreation Area

N

TENNESSEE

Winston-Salem

Great Smoky Mountains
National Park

Raleigh

Little Tennessee
River

NORTH
CAROLINA

Springer
Mtn.

SOUTH CAROLINA

Savannah

Columbia

GEORGIA

0   50   100

Distance in miles

THE APPALACHIAN TRAIL, THE WORLD'S LONGEST FOOTPATH, slinks for more than twenty-one hundred miles over mountaintops, ridge lines, valley floors, wildflower meadows, isolated cow pastures, and a few paved roads, all remote but within shouting distance of one hundred million people along the American East Coast. The exact trail length is never certain, as the A.T. is rerouted each year to get as far away from civilization as possible. Besides, how does one precisely measure a path that scrambles over rocks, tree roots, big and little bridges, a few fences, and such natural features as "the Lemon Squeezer," "the Priest," "Pollywog Stream," "Eph's Lookout," "the Pinnacle," "Crawfish Valley," "Hogwallow Spring," "Dragon's Tooth," "Beauty Spot," "Charlies Bunion," and "the Guillotine"?

The north-south trail connects fourteen states from Maine to Georgia, but it runs east-westerly in spots, especially in New England where the A.T. was hacked through forestland to connect existing north-south trails in Maine, New Hampshire, and Vermont. Several New England sections follow trails like the Long Trail and "Fishin' Jimmy Trail" that existed well before the footpath from Maine to Georgia was conceived. The Appalachian Mountain Club, the first known hiking club, was founded in 1876 "to explore the mountains of New England and adjacent regions for both scientific and artistic purposes."

The trail hugs the crestline of the ancient, wrinkled Appalachian Mountains, named by Spanish explorer Hernando de Soto after the Appalachee Indians who lived in northwest Florida. Trails of the southern Appalachians were cut by buffalo that roamed the land before European settlement. Early adventurers and botanists were thrilled to discover the bounty of flowering plants and shrubs of the Appalachians, notably mountain laurel, flame azalea, and rhododendron. They saw literally billions of chestnut trees that have since gone—victims of a terrible blight. Today another plague, acid rain, appears to be killing or damaging southern Fraser firs.

The Appalachians are old, worn-out mountains by American standards and were formed by staggering geological compressions and uplifts. A.T. thru hikers must conquer almost all of their most daunting peaks, including Clingmans Dome in North Carolina (6,643 feet)—the second-highest—and soaring Mount Washington in New Hampshire (6,288 feet). But much of the trail's course worms under a dense canopy of trees—a "tunnel through time," as *National Geographic* called the trail in 1987. Rivers have sliced several gaps through the mountains, and A.T. hikers traverse those as well.

The idea of an Appalachian Trail was proposed in an article published in the obscure *Journal of the American Institute of Architects* in 1921 by Benton MacKaye, a Yankee forester, hiker, dreamer, and believer in the "creative value of wilderness." It was written at a time when "tramping," as hiking was known, was becoming a passion among many New England intellectuals. According to the member handbook of the Appalachian Trail Conference, the governing body of most trail activities, "the article proposed an extended wilderness along the Appalachian crests as a crucial line of defense against both demoralization of urban laborers (by providing a refuge for contemplation in a natural setting) and 'the lure of militarism' (by channeling primal heroic instincts into the care of the countryside)."

The A.T. idea was peddled to supportive newspaper columnists and outdoor enthusiasts, including the national commissioner of the Boy Scouts of America. Hiking clubs joined in the fun of proposing the trail's exact route, and the first section was cut and christened at the Palisades

In 1989, Girl Scout leader and two-thousand-miler Mary Sands of Louisville, Kentucky, began the twelve-inch patches of this quilt (opposite)—representing all fourteen Appalachian Trail states—at her quilting workshop at Appalachian Trail Conference headquarters in Harpers Ferry, West Virginia. She gave the A.T.C. the completed masterpiece a year later.

Interstate Park in New York in 1922. A bridge there had made a connection between New England and the New York–New Jersey area—and thence southward—possible.

At the trail's official organizing conference at the Hotel Raleigh in Washington, D.C., in 1925, attendees agreed upon an Appalachian Trail monogram, in which the crossbar of the *A* serves as the top of the *T*. The logo is in use to this day. At the conference, MacKaye was careful to distinguish between his "trailway" and a railway. He said a railway opens the countryside to civilization but "the trailway should 'open up' a country as an escape from civilization." Later, he would write that "the Appalachian Range should be placed in public hands and become the site for a Barbarian Utopia."

Others like Myron H. Avery, A.T.C. chairman from 1931 to 1952—a legend in hiking circles unknown in the greater society—turned MacKaye's lofty vision into a reality. What would be designated America's first National Scenic Trail thirty-one years later was completed from Mount Katahdin in central Maine to Mount Oglethorpe in northern Georgia with the opening of the south slope of Mount Sugarloaf, Maine, in 1937. A year later, an unnamed, devastating hurricane that killed hundreds of people and destroyed whole coastal villages in New England nearly obliterated the trail in that region. At the time there were no more than one hundred active volunteers on the entire length of the trail—compared with more than forty-five hundred today—ready to effect repairs.

The Appalachian Trail crossed this Virginia mountain dweller's property when the Blue Ridge Parkway was under construction. According to the photographer, "he does not like anyone *with a uniform."*

Of the fifteen hundred eager people who depart Springer Mountain in Georgia or Mount Katahdin in Maine, determined to hike the trail's entire distance in a calendar year, an estimated three hundred make it. Four-fifths or more of thru hikers travel south to north (GA>ME in hiker parlance), most leaving Springer in the early spring in hopes of missing the worst of southern summertime heat and northern early-fall chills. Fewer hike north to south because they must wait for the Mount Katahdin snow thaw. Most years, Baxter State Park rangers won't even *allow* thru hikers to depart from Katahdin until June 1 or thereafter.

Awarding of a patch for completing the trail—the only reward beyond satisfaction—is strictly on the honor system. No longer does a panel of experienced hikers grill a purported

successful thru hiker, as was the case for the first twenty-five years or more, to be sure he or she hiked the entire way. Earl Shaffer of York, Pennsylvania, faced such an "oral comprehensive" exam—and had to show his series of slides taken all along the route—when he became the first documented person to hike the entire trail in 1948. Only well-wishers and photographers greeted him in Maine when he repeated the hike in 1998 at age seventy-nine—lugging the same tiny backpack—to mark the fiftieth anniversary of the feat.

The Earl Shaffer of 1998 was older than most, but not all, hikers. Don Cogswell, owner of both a diner and a lodge catering to hikers in Millinocket, Maine, once ran into an eighty-two-year-old man who asked for a lift to the start of the trail at Baxter State Park. "His trail name was 'Papa,'" Cogswell says. "I took him out to the mountain. He looked through the windshield and said, 'Don, I can't wait to tackle it.' I said, 'Papa, I don't want to be disrespectful, but you're a freak of nature!'"

Trail names are a relatively recent phenomenon. A.T.C. officials trace them to the 1970s when clever C.B.-radio "handles" were in vogue. Many hikers on the Appalachian Trail introduce, and forever

Forester, inveterate hiker, and futurist philosopher Emile Benton MacKaye first proposed the concept of an Appalachian Trail in 1921. He visualized a "long-distance footway" as an inspiring "second world."

know, each other by their trail names alone. Some have even had their names legally changed to their trail personas. "There's an element of fantasy in the thru-hiking experience," says Brian King, A.T.C. public-affairs director. Another badge of identity and individuality among hikers is the walking stick, often carved with care by a loving relative.

One does not really *walk* the Appalachian Trail. Nor is it a hike in the image of a happy wanderer, whistling along a gently sloping path. Neither, however, is conquering the A.T. an extreme sport, akin to rappelling. Rather, one could be said to *trudge* the trail in five million or more strides, purposefully and carefully under a considerable burden. Even frugally stuffed backpacks weigh forty pounds. Among the packed items considered essential: a bandanna, lip salve, water filters or iodine tablets, a candle, a waterproof pack cover, and "mountain money"—toilet paper. And, of course, some folding money, a credit card, and at least a dollar's worth of change.

Jagged and slippery rocks, exposed roots, and muddy ruts await the hiker's step. There are treacherous jumps across boulders and grades that can be steep. To many hikers' surprise, the jaunt *down* a mountainside can be far more grueling than the trip up because of the pounding to feet and knees. Surprisingly, too, hikers soon loathe the stretches along hard, smooth roads and bridges, preferring the softer footfall of the earthen trail.

Many unfortunate thru hikers must cope with steady rain and the attendant mud. In *A Walk in the Woods*—an often hilarious account of his hike of 870 miles of the A.T. in 1996—Bill Bryson, a travel writer from Hanover, New Hampshire, recalled:

Mud became a feature of our lives. We trudged through it, stumbled and fell through it, knelt in it, set our packs down in it, left a streak of it on everything we touched. And always when you moved there was the maddening, monotonous sound of your nylon going *wiss, wiss, wiss* until you wanted to take a gun and shoot it.

Before the Appalachian Trail could be rerouted through woodland, it traversed some less than breathtaking stretches. It is thought that this is the rubble of an old manganese mine near Marion, Virginia.

Whether or not it was raining, Bryson points out that he and his companion—like all A.T. thru hikers—walked farther every twenty minutes than most Americans walk in a week. Thanks to generally sturdier boots and lots of practice, successful thru hikers find a comfortable gait that enables them to hike ten, fifteen, even twenty miles in a day. It is thought that the record for traversing the entire trail in a season is fifty-two days, nine hours, forty-one minutes, held by David "the Runner" Horton of Lynchburg, Virginia. Needless to say, he hiked fast, slept little, and traveled light! A year earlier Bill "Orient Express" Irwin had become the first blind hiker to cover the whole trail.

Thru hikers soon discover the delights, obstacles, and eccentricities of the trail including seventy straight miles of crestline in the Great Smoky Mountains; spectacular bridge crossings of great rivers, including the Shenandoah, Potomac, and Delaware; a pleasant stroll through abandoned hillside farmlands in Vermont; and a long stretch above the timberline in New Hampshire's Presidential Range where snowstorms pop up every month of the year.

The last miles of a south-to-north thru hike are often the most remarked-upon. Enervated hikers must leave Monson, Maine, and traverse the "Hundred-mile Wilderness," which is devoid of roads or towns, before arriving at Abol Bridge over the Penobscot River, near the final stretch in Baxter State Park. Five or six Yellowstone National Parks could fit inside this virtually uninhabited Wilderness, which has never been formally surveyed. And then there is the last, taxing climb of Mount Katahdin, where late-summer afternoon thunderstorms, pierced by dangerous lightning arrays, are legend.

Almost as daunting as the physical challenge of the Appalachian Trail is the boredom that sets in. Brilliant sunsets, grazing deer, arresting fog banks, and spectacular valley views quickly lose their allure as the "grind" of a twenty-one-hundred-mile trek sets in. Homesickness intrudes, too. "Are you willing to plod up seemingly endless mountains with muscles that ache, only to see another grind still to come?" asks the A.T.C. of prospective thru hikers in one of its pamphlets. Some of the best-conditioned hikers are the first to drop off the trail when they lack the self-sufficiency and *inner* strength to keep going. As simple an impediment as a single foot blister can send a perfect physical specimen packing. Twenty percent of hikers who begin the trail intending to reach the distant terminus drop out within the first ten days. Some heading north abandon hope even *before* they start the trail, because the eight-mile "approach trail" from Georgia's Amicalola State Park up Springer Mountain to the A.T. starting point is so daunting.

No demographic figures can be kept, but the A.T.C. estimates that one-third of all thru hikers are college-age men and women, often just out of school and awaiting their first jobs. Another third are retirees who have the time and determination to attempt the long journey. The remainder, of all ages, are changing jobs, get sabbaticals, or have a hefty nest egg—necessary because the reasonably equipped thru hiker will spend $5,000 or $6,000 on gear, clothes, and food.

Parents of some hikers—and, secretly, some thru hikers themselves—worry about bears, snakes, criminals, or frightening encounters with drooling backwoodsmen of the sort depicted in the dark movie *Deliverance*. Statistics are faulty because many incidents go unreported, but the Appalachian Trail Conference calculates that a half-dozen or so hikers—many day hikers who are intoxicated—die on the A.T. each year, often from sunstroke, heart attacks, or falls. There have been close calls, but no reported deaths, over twenty-five years ending in 1998 from hypothermia following late-spring blizzards. There have been no snake bites of humans (though some of pet dogs who tag along). There has been much sickness but no deaths from drinking untreated water. And over the twenty-five-year period, there have been seven known murders of hikers, a like number of rapes, and numerous thefts of backpacks. The biggest crime problem associated with the trail is the vandalism of cars while their owners are off day hiking.

Broadway actor Walter Greene helped blaze the Appalachian Trail through the "Wilderness" from Baxter State Park to Monson, Maine. Hikers there must carry ten days' worth of food because they cannot resupply.

To reduce confrontations with unsavory locals, A.T. officials have moved the trail farther off roads and away from picnic areas and other "beer party" locations where hikers are apt to get hassled. Hunting is permitted over many sections of the trail, but no hiker has been shot during the long reporting period. In Georgia, Army Rangers practice in the mountains, popping out from the trees in forbidding camouflage gear, but they are under strict instructions not to bother hikers.

Long-distance hikers report developing a keen "woods sense" that allows them to detect potential trouble from humans or animals. Most fellow hikers prove to be eminently honest and trustworthy, and criminals are usually too clumsy or lazy to venture far off the road. For protection and constant companionship, some thru hikers take along the family dog. This is strongly discouraged as the mutts slow down progress (by regulation, they must be leashed) and are far more likely to rile a snake, fox, moose, or bear than is a hiker.

Many an otherwise fit hiker has had to retire from the trail after breaking an ankle or tearing up a knee. Another hiker will normally

In 1934, newspaper publisher Warner Hall struck the pose that became the model for the Georgia Appalachian Trail Club's marker plaque—shown on page 1—sculpted by club member George Noble.

come upon the fallen traveler, make him or her as comfortable as possible, and go for help. Sometimes other hikers come along and construct a makeshift litter to get the person to a road and ultimate rescue. But in rugged back country, such as the formidable White Mountains, rescue parties of fifty or more must be quickly organized to evacuate victims by forming human chains.

Officially the Appalachian Trail is overseen by the National Park Service, although only a single ranger, operating out of Harpers Ferry, West Virginia—approximately one hundred miles to the south of the midpoint of the trail—assumes that responsibility. The park service also assigns a small staff of specialists to the trail in matters such as land acquisition and environmental impact.

The park service delegates the running of the trail to a caretaker organization, the Appalachian Trail Conference, also headquartered in Harpers Ferry, with regional offices in Pennsylvania, New Hampshire, Virginia, and North Carolina. The budget of the A.T.C. exceeds $3 million. It is raised from membership dues, a hefty federal payment, foundation and corporate support, and income from the conference's maps, guidebooks, and other publications.

The A.T.C. faces one tricky but amusing problem: how to pronounce its name! Headquarters is located just below the Mason-Dixon line, where the preference is "Appa-LATCH-ian. In the North and elsewhere, it's commonly "Appa-LAY-shin" or "Appa-LAY-chin." Most often, A.T.C. personnel answer the telephone with one of the "Yankee" pronunciations.

Approximately 40 percent of the Appalachian Trail winds through national parks, and another 40 percent through national forests. The remainder traverses state-owned land or, in increasingly shorter stretches, towns or private property. But the trail would not exist without the direct involvement of thirty-one hiking clubs, each of which accepts responsibility for a section of the trail. Some of these clubs are located quite far from the trail. The Tidewater, Virginia, organization, for instance, meets in and around Norfolk, 250 miles from its ten-mile trail section in south-central Virginia. Some clubs have active members as far away as Michigan who drive east once or twice a year to help maintain a part of the trail. All told, trail volunteers spend 175,000 or more hours a year keeping the Appalachian Trail as pristine as possible.

Overall on paper, the trail's cooperative management arrangement looks like a Rube Goldberg affair of 250 overlapping jurisdictions. But bureaucratic gridlock is avoided for one simple reason: There is no time for turf wars or theoretical disputes; there is too much work to be done, each and every month, in the field.

One organizational challenge, not well resolved, involves the increasing commercialization of the trail. Bakeries, cafés, outfitters, and hostels are quick to attach their identities to the trail. A Tennessee department store even successfully trademarked an "Appalachian Trail" brand of clothes. There are many privately published trail guidebooks and at least one pricey guide service that offers to tag along on the edges of a client's thru hike, meeting him or her at a road crossing every night, bringing good food every night and driving the hiker to a motel or comfortable campground. This experience is hardly "roughing it."

The Appalachian Trail Conference faces a continuing conundrum. Its mission is to manage, protect, and *promote* the trail at the same time. It publishes trail guides, maps, and newsletters; registers and photographs thru hikers as they reach Harpers Ferry; and operates two Internet web sites. This all attracts more hikers to the trail, making it harder to protect and keep wild. The contradiction is eased when trail managers remind themselves that an estimated four million day hikers and other "short timers" a year hike the trail in small stretches. Thru hikers need more attention and services over a five- to seven-month period, but recreational hikers deserve a memorable visit to the trail as well.

Still, it is thru hikers who are the stuff of legend on the Appalachian Trail. The following recounts a few of their stories.

Nineteen-year-old Kyra Dotter was an unlikely candidate to even start hiking the Appalachian Trail, let alone finish it. She was working as a medical technician near her home in California's Mojave Desert. Scrawny in stature, she had rollerbladed and dabbled in aerobics but had never hiked anywhere, not even "car camped" overnight. It was a confusing time in her life. Rings pierced many parts of her body. Partial to the color purple, this pale young woman wore purple nail polish, purple lipstick, purple makeup. Little wonder, when she began to hike the A.T. in Georgia in early 1997, another hiker gave her the trail name "Purple Haze."

Kyra had picked up one of her brother's books, *Appalachian Adventure*, and when he and three of his friends announced that they were going to hike the trail, she shocked them all by asking to go along.

Conditioning would not prove to be a problem. "The trail gets you in shape," she says. At first she averaged just five miles a day, but was doing fifteen or twenty by the time she reached West Virginia. Amazingly, within three months her companions had all quit and gone home.

Catherine Robbins, Hilda Kurth, and Kathleen Norris, left to right, were the first women to hike Vermont's 260-mile Long Trail in 1927— shown here taking an occasional rest and ukulele break.

Purple Haze almost did, too. Her feet, knees, and hips ached. Her Achilles' tendons were painfully stretched. Her one-person tent collapsed on top of her. Mold grew inside her rain jacket. Once she was briefly trapped when her foot got caught in a crevice. "Mentally, you feel you're done," she remembers. "Or physically, like when I was having foot problems and I got covered with bug bites. I had blisters everywhere. I looked like this horrible diseased mess. I was sick to my stomach. But I walked until I couldn't walk any more."

But Purple Haze did not quit. She used the solitude to test the limits of her endurance, and to look inside herself. A vegetarian, she missed vegetables and fresh fruit. Eating starchy food for strength, she says, "was awful. But you're not going to carry a big head of lettuce and three cucumbers and six apples, because they're going to weigh so much with all the water in them."

The greater world outside the trail "just did not exist" for Purple Haze. "After a while," she says, "you think, this is what I do. I walk." Indeed, many successful hikers report a remarkable metamorphosis. Striding through the endless forest, they are no longer students or secretaries or homemakers. They are hikers. Many report an incredibly difficult transition back into the "real world" of responsibilities and relationships when their thru hikes are completed. Disoriented, many take odd jobs and continue hiking the A.T. or other trails again and again.

After she completed the trail in seven months and seventeen days, Kyra Dotter returned to California. She moved to San Francisco but soon missed the green and quietude of the eastern mountains, missed hiking and hikers. So, minus the gaudy purple outfits and body rings, she returned east to work at a restaurant frequented by thru-hikers near the trail in Millinocket, Maine. Its name, fittingly: The Appalachian Trail Café.

Twenty-eight-year-old Janet Offermann was weary of her stress-filled job as an actuarial analyst in Richmond, Virginia, when she decided to attempt to walk the Appalachian Trail in 1996. An avid runner, she was in good physical shape but deliberately put on eight to ten pounds before beginning the journey, knowing she would lose weight on the trail. As predicted, she would arrive in Maine thirty pounds lighter than she left Georgia.

Offermann—trail name "Interplanet Janet" after an energetic television cartoon character—began the journey with seven companions from other regions; she had met them by correspondence through a trail newsletter. Only two, a man nicknamed "Allgood" and a woman named "Marmot," completed the trek, not always hiking together but usually catching up with one another at shelters at day's end.

"I expected it to be much more strenuous, much riskier, than it turned out to be," Janet says. "I expected bears. Didn't see a single one, except in captivity at Bear Mountain Zoo (right on the trail) in New York." She grew comfortable in the woods and terribly uneasy in trail towns. "Crossing streets, the cars, the lights seemed a lot more dangerous," she says. "The worst stretch was Pennsylvania, going over rocks day after day. I still remember waking up, and my feet would still be sore from the day before, then having to walk on sore feet over even more rocks."

Her parents sent her provisions, which Janet had pre-packed. "I got sick of oatmeal," she says. "I told my mom to take it out and put in Pop Tarts instead." The provisions included clean underwear and T-shirts; a cellular phone, which rarely worked in the remote highlands; a small cooking stove, which Interplanet Janet soon sent home, preferring trail mix and cold sandwiches; and moleskin, intended to cover blisters. "I ended up just popping the blisters with a safety pin," she recalls. "Not very sanitary, but it worked."

Offermann was never bored or distracted, she says. "It was a kind of meditative experience, living for the moment. I did feel for a time that my mind was kind of deadened, so I'd read a book in the shelters." She was surprised when she finally reached trail's end atop Mount Katahdin "that it wasn't this big, elated moment. Instead it was like, 'OK, I'm at the end of the trail, and in a few moments I'll be hiking down the mountain'" and going home. "I was glad, but there was so much calmness in me that I didn't need some big exciting moment." Nor did she report "hiker's appetite," a common experience among those who complete the trail.

Overall, Interplanet Janet "got a lot of inner peace from it, a lot more perspective. Now, when things get harried, I can bring myself back to the trail and kind of get that trail calm back." It took her two to three months after getting home, she says, to lose the stoop in her stride from carrying a heavy backpack (as Bill Bryson notes in *A Walk in the Woods*, "it is one thing to walk 2,000 miles, quite another to walk 2,000 miles with a wardrobe on your back"), and even longer to adjust to the noise of urban life. She found herself talking less, listening more, watching almost no television. She switched jobs to a position with less pressure, still hikes and helps her local trail club maintain its section of the trail, and keeps in touch with Allgood and Marmot, both of whom she is certain will be friends for life.

Hilton "Buddy" Newell of Whitefield, New Hampshire, was fifty-five and just retired as a postmaster in 1989. He had hiked a little with his family and knew many thru hikers who would use his post office as a "drop site" for provisions sent from home. Sometimes he would

Trailblazers follow Myron Avery, the U.S. Maritime Commission lawyer who was the first A.T.C. chairman, as he pushes a measuring wheel up rocky Hunt Spur of Mount Katahdin.

invite hikers home for a hot meal, shower, and a night in a clean, warm bed. That is how Newell's son, Randy, a high-school student, became infatuated with the idea of hiking the Appalachian Trail.

But Randy Newell contracted multiple sclerosis. As his condition worsened, he was confined to a wheelchair and eventually bed. "So I told him I'd be, I guess you'd call it, a 'surrogate hiker,'" says Buddy Newell. There he was, one day in April 1989, atop Springer Mountain, with his daughter Diane, about to challenge the Appalachian Trail. His granddaughter, Nicole, would join them later. Their trail names were "The Three G's" for three generations.

But only Buddy made it to Maine.

He took with him a mini-tape recorder on which to detail the events of each day. When he would reach a post office, he would mail the tapes home to Randy. "That way," says Newell, "he could do the trail. It's basically what kept me out there." He sent home stories of the aches and pains, of the meager food and new, fast friends, of the copperhead snake that slithered up his foot while he napped, or the rattlesnake that he stepped over, thinking it was a fallen branch, of the odd sensation of watching a passing car after several days in the woods, when a scampering squirrel was the fastest object he had seen, or of the crazy things that preoccupy the mind in the woods. "You become almost insane with weight," he says. "Our whole group cut off toothbrush handles. We'd get toilet tissue and knock the core out. You'll do anything to lessen the weight." It is a tale confirmed by every thru hiker.

Through his father, Randy Newell "walked" the trail vicariously. He listened to taped entries like this, about an injured hiker:

The 1923 Long Trail Lodge atop Sherburne Pass in Killington, Vermont, was a Green Mountain hikers' oasis. After a fire in 1968, activities moved to an annex that became the Inn at Long Trail.

Troy had fallen, and with his left foot facing the wrong way lay there in such pain that he had not even been able to move enough to remove his pack. He was shivering badly, so Kenny covered him with a sleeping bag and ran the distance back to the road to find a telephone. Soon the emergency medical technician unit was there and removed him from the trail to the local hospital in Tennessee. The three of us spent a sad night in the shelter, as Troy had become "family."

Once, in Maryland, Newell and his companions came upon a trip wire across the trail. It was hooked to a hidden U.S. Army bomb simulator. "Packed a pretty good punch, would have blown our legs off," he says. Newell disarmed it and proceeded north, intending to notify the next authority figure he could find, only to run into a fellow with a shotgun aimed directly at him, his daughter, and granddaughter. "The girls both started crying," he says. "I said we should walk straight ahead like we didn't see the guy. So we did, cringing, waiting for the gun to go off, which it never did." Two days later he found a ranger, who thanked him for the alert and informed Newell "there had been some survivalists reported in the area."

"I'd never been a quitter," Buddy Newell says, "but I would have quit if I'd not been hiking for other reasons. Had there been a bus stop near me at several points . . . " His voice trails off. "You know, you're wet for seven, eight days in a row. The only dry clothes you have is the set you sleep in. You get up in the morning and have to put the wet clothes back on again. It's very unpleasant. You get a week of this, and it's enough to make anyone wonder, 'Why am I doing this?'"

He knew why, of course. He was doing it for Randy, who would die of his debilitating disease a few years later. Could Buddy Newell do it again? Physically, yes, he says. Psychologically, he is not sure.

There would be no such unforgettable experiences for the Purple Hazes, Interplanet Janets, and Three G's of the Appalachian Trail without the volunteer labor of "maintainers" from each of the trail clubs. Fran Leckie, for instance, joined the Old Dominion Appalachian Trail Club, based in Richmond—a two-hour drive from the club's 17.4-mile section of the trail in central Virginia—in 1992. She and two friends had hiked every inch of the Virginia portion of the trail in small bites on weekend day trips. That took time, as one-fourth of the A.T. lies in Virginia. With her trail repair work today, she says, "I wanted to say thanks for the beauty for the pleasure I got from it, wanted to pay back the people who created the trail and kept it up for all of us."

Four years later, Leckie was in charge of the trail maintenance crews for the Old Dominion club. Once a month, every month, in sleet, snow, pouring rain, or summer steam, she and a dozen or so other volunteers report to a picnic area near Humpback Rocks. Tools are kept in a shed there—picks, shovels, chain saws, rock bars, Weed Whackers. Many workers prefer the simpler, old-fashioned tools because they are easier to carry into and out of the deep woods. Their task is to keep the footpath four feet wide, with at least an eight-foot-high clearance to accommodate the ever-increasing height of hikers' backpacks.

Once every two or three years, the maintainers freshen the two-inch by six-inch white-painted blazes that mark the Appalachian Trail. Two blazes atop each other signal an obscure turn and alert hikers to consult their trail maps before proceeding. Blue blazes mark side trails,

Early Appalachian Trail Conferences like this gathering at Daicey Pond in Maine in 1939 focused on building the trail. The conference grew into both a permanent management organization and a biennial gathering.

Conditions were primitive when Earl Shaffer became the first verified thru hiker of the Appalachian Trail in 1948. Stories in National Geographic about the hike, and his own book, inspired others to copy him.

viewpoints, campsites, and shelters—if you can call the 250 nighttime stopping places shelters. Most are little more than three-sided lean-tos, invariably open to the elements on the side from which rain, snow, or cold winds are advancing. There is usually an elevated board that serves as a crude loft on which hikers can lay their sleeping bags, sometimes a picnic table or a "bear pole" from which to hang food, and little else. The shelter floor is often wet, muddy, littered, and miserable. Fortunately there are inexpensive boarding houses, old hotels, and hostels—some, like Bears Den in Northern Virginia, run by the A.T.C. itself—not far off the trail at several points along the Appalachian Trail.

Blazes replaced axe marks—which sometimes killed trees—and metal diamonds tacked to trees and posts. The diamonds are now collectors' items. There is no set distance apart for blazes. Where the trail is well worn and relatively flat, they may be as much as a ten-minute walk apart—well out of eyeshot from each other. In heavily wooded or tricky locations involving intersecting trails, turns, or road crossings, however, the standard is that one should be able to stand at the spot of one blaze and see the next one in the distance. The blazes are as unobtrusive as possible, as this is supposed to be back country; the handiwork of man is to be kept to a minimum.

Trail maintainers have many natural enemies: simple overgrowth in the summertime; erosion that can turn the trail into an impassable gully; ice storms that break off the tops of trees, depositing them directly onto the trail; and even occasional hurricanes, such as (ironically) Hurricane Fran in 1996. Fran toppled more than one hundred trees across the path in a 7.5-mile stretch of the Old Dominion club's territory.

To address the erosion problem, crews dig pits in the trail into which they roll small boulders arduously pried from the nearby woods. The newly placed rocks protrude a few inches from the ground, but they are less of a hazard than holes and exposed roots. "We do this to get out into nature, to meet wonderful people, to feel the satisfaction of doing something useful with your hands," Fran Leckie says. "Many of us would rather do trail work than hike." It is a story repeated thirty-one times over in each club's section of the Appalachian Trail. Maintainers are doctors, carpenters, retired physicists, grateful former thru-hikers of all ages, even unemployed laborers. There are no social distinctions on the Appalachian Trail.

Over the years almost the entire length of the trail—nearly two thousand miles' worth—has been relocated to get the trail off roads, out of cities and subdivisions, and onto public land in the woods. As late as 1968, when President Lyndon Johnson signed the National Trails Act, roughly half the Appalachian Trail was located on private lands or roads, some of which were paved and heavily traveled. Thereafter, where possible, the trail was moved not only deeper into the woods but also higher to realize Benton MacKaye's vision of a "ridgecrest trail" with a view—a walk on top of the world. Even in states like Connecticut and New Jersey that have limited high ground, planners go for what height they can find. Since 1968 the Federal Government has purchased more than four thousand different tracts of land in places not already in national parks or forests. When agreement cannot be reached on a price, seizure is by eminent domain. In some cases, as in the Cumberland Valley of Pennsylvania, previous landowners are allowed to continue to farm or graze cattle on a ridge, so hikers can experience walking through a pasture or cornfield. (The grazing of bulls is not permitted!)

In Central Virginia, Fran Leckie's crews worked to move a section of trail deeper into the woods. Whole busloads of day hikers, even tourists, had discovered the same picnic area where the club stores its tools and had begun tramping down the A.T. on raucous excursions. Nearby, Virginia's Skyline Drive—whose route *was* the Appalachian Trail before a paved road supplanted it—is inundated with picnickers and "leaf peepers" each weekend. The A.T. crosses Skyline Drive thirty-seven times and passes, in some places, directly below overlooks. Fortunately for A.T. hikers, side trails leading to waterfalls and other natural attractions have proved more appealing to casual hikers, and Appalachian Trail hikers can navigate Skyline Drive through Shenandoah National Park with surprisingly little interference. One thing is for sure: Unlike the experience on some of the newer western trails, including one over the Continental Divide, hiking the A.T. will never be a true "wilderness experience." One cannot hope to go days or weeks before bumping into other hikers.

To alleviate overcrowding caused by the bunching up of hikers starting out in Georgia each spring, the Appalachian Trail Conference encourages section hiking (in which hikers complete the trail, but in stages, sometimes over several years), or "flip-flopping." Flip-floppers typically hike north to a point at which they realize they will not make Mount Katahdin before it is closed for the winter. So they catch a ride to Maine and work their way south to the point where they had left the trail. Some gluttons for punishment "yo-yo" the full trail, hiking one direction first (usually north), then immediately heading back the entire way in the opposite direction. In 1982–1983, Steve Nuckolls completed three thru hikes, from Georgia to Maine to Georgia to Maine, in a row; and in 1984, Phil Goad accomplished the same feat in one calendar year.

The A.T. has its distinctive social protocols: the inventive trail names, courteous sharing of limited shelter and hostel space, and communication via journals at points along the trail. This "A.T. Internet" is little more than a series of crude spiral notebooks filled with handwritten, often banal, entries: "Passed Cooter en route to Beagle Gap"; "Saw tons of deer but no bears. Bummer"; "Another glorious day to be alive!"; "Take my advice learned the hard way. Don't bother using the bear pole."

Shaffer took copious photographs and notes when he first hiked the trail. He repeated the trip in 1965 and again— to mark the first hike's fiftieth anniversary—in 1998 at age seventy-nine.

The journals are the trail lifeline. They are the first place authorities check to determine the last movements of missing hikers. The F.B.I. has even irritated A.T.C. officials by occasionally confiscating journals as when it searched for Atlanta Olympic bombing suspect Eric Rudolph in the North Carolina mountains in the late 1990s.

While the Appalachian Trail is intended to be a far-off-road route along which to commune with nature, the trail enters, or closely passes, dozens of little towns. Little places like Oquossoc, Maine; Etna, New Hampshire; Peru, Vermont; Delaware Water Gap, Pennsylvania; Bland, Virginia; and Helen, Georgia, provide welcome access to a hot shower, a laundromat, a good meal, a snug bed, and friendly people. Indeed, each trail town is famous among hikers for its "trail magic" kindnesses that sympathetic "trail angels" accord.

Each town has its own local color, as well.

Dahlonega, Georgia, for instance, near the southern terminus, was the site of "gold fever" in the 1820s after gold nuggets were found in Yahoola Creek.

In Erwin, Tennessee, "Murderous Mary," a circus elephant, killed

her trainer at a performance in 1916. Townsfolk shot her, but when she did not die she was allowed to perform at a show that night! The next day, residents took her to the railroad yard and hanged the ponderous pachyderm from a crane. Later, they found that Mary had an abscessed tooth that might have provoked her rampage.

Damascus, Virginia, just across the Tennessee border, is a welcome sight after long days high atop the Smoky Mountains. Since 1987, Damascus has set out to prove it is the "Friendliest Town on the Trail" by throwing a four-day Appalachian Trail festival. The event has become a favorite thru-hikers' reunion, and new hikers who left Georgia in early March arrive just in time to enjoy the festivities as well.

Five great American generals are associated with the history of Lexington, Virginia. George Washington donated money to save the local college from closing. Robert E. Lee would one day become its president. Stonewall Jackson taught at Virginia Military Institute, which both George Patton and George Marshall attended.

It was in Harpers Ferry, then in Virginia, that Kansas firebrand John Brown came to raid an armory in 1859, seeking guns to mount a slave rebellion; captured and hanged by Federal troops led by Colonel Robert E. Lee, Brown became a martyr for the abolitionist cause.

Pine Grove Furnace, Pennsylvania, was the center of a thriving charcoal iron industry from colonial times past the Civil War; a blacksmith shop near the state park there is a museum today.

Woodstock, Vermont, is routinely counted among the five most beautiful towns in America. No telephone or electric wires run above ground here. It has a quintessential New England green and a massive 1793 hotel. Most homes are original as is the town's famous apple pie.

Bretton Woods, New Hampshire, on a plateau below Mount Washington, was the site of a world monetary conference in 1945 that led to the establishment of the World Bank and International Monetary Fund. The nation's only steam-powered cog railway chugs up the mountain right past A.T. hikers.

There is actually a fixed, permanent route for the Appalachian Trail, if only on maps. Developed by volunteer clubs, the National Park Service, the U.S. Forest Service, and the A.T.C., it

Emma "Grandma" Gatewood, hiking in Keds sneakers and carrying a fourteen-pound bag over her shoulder, became the first woman to complete the trail alone in one continuous trip in 1956.

was published in the Federal Register in 1981. The federal government has spent more than $175 million acquiring land to make this trail a reality as well as millions more marking the trail's boundaries about five hundred feet to each side of the route, so landowners, hunters, and developers will know when they are encroaching.

Recent biennial meetings of the Appalachian Trail Conference have come to represent the nation's largest nonprofit gatherings of conservationists. Well over one thousand people have registered for each—in telling contrast to the ninth A.T.C. gathering, attended by sixty-eight diehard hikers in 1939.

The organization has increasingly fixed its sights on the future of the great footpath. With the goal at hand of having the entire Appalachian Trail on public land, conferees could herald the day that Benton MacKaye and Myron Avery's vision of a continuous and protected route through the eastern mountains was becoming a reality.

But the celebration carries an ironic challenge: how to deal with *overuse* by casual users? It's a concern that was manifest in the very theme of the 1997 A.T.C. gathering outside Bethel, Maine, sixty miles

Until the National Park Service began acquiring backcountry through which to re-route the Appalachian Trail, parts of the trail wound through decidedly unrustic settings like this sub-division in the 1970s.

and sixty years removed from the place where the trail was completed in 1937. That theme: "Loving the Trail to Death."

Is there such a thing as overuse? Is not the surge in trail use an opportunity as well as a management problem? In his column in the *Appalachian Trailway News,* David B. Field, chairman of the Appalachian Trail Conference, wrote in late 1997, "'Overuse' is a value-loaded term, implying some kind of 'bad' condition.... There is simply no absolute intrinsic 'goodness' or 'badness' associated with any Trail-management practice or Trail-use activity." One person's value judgment that the trail is being overused, he added, may not square with another's view that the more hiking of the Appalachian Trail, the better. "It is a mistake to try to debate" these differing perceptions of appropriate trail use, Field concluded.

Surely, the ever-growing popularity of the Appalachian Trail will strain the resources of the volunteers who are the backbone of this treasured scenic trail.

Bill Bryson points out that the Appalachian Trail has already outlasted the Oregon and Santa Fe trails, the coast-to-coast Lincoln Highway, and old U.S. Route 66. Today there is talk of an "International Appalachian Trail." More than talk, actually. Work is proceeding to connect a trail that reaches nearly to the top of the Appalachian chain on Quebec's Gaspé Peninsula to the A.T. at the Abol Bridge below Mount Katahdin in Maine. Down south, there is work apace to extend the trail nearly to Birmingham, Alabama, and another proposal to run a trail clear to the Florida Everglades. But unless legislation is changed, the route of the Appalachian Trail itself will not be changed.

On the other hand, because nature bedevils the trail each winter, and each hiker's experience is unique come spring, it is the attitude of trail administrators, volunteers, and hikers alike that the Appalachian National Scenic Trail will never be finished.

A plaque (above) atop Springer Mountain in Georgia marks the Appalachian Trail's starting point—or for southbound thru hikers, finish. It contains no words of inspiration but rather historical information. The path down Springer (opposite) looks harmless, but slips on loose stones and rocky ledges end many a novice hiker's dreams just as their adventures are beginning. In Cherokee mythology, Blood Mountain at Neels Gap (overleaf) was home to a race of Spirit People.

Only once in more than twenty-one hundred miles—at the Walasi Yi Center in Georgia (above)—does the Appalachian Trail go through a building. The center (right) was built by President Roosevelt's Civilian Conservation Corps as an inn and tea room in 1937. Its snacks, backpacking gear, clean restrooms, and friendly faces are a welcome sight to hikers who have picked up their first blisters in the thirty-mile tramp from Springer Mountain.

NEEL GAP
ELEVATION 3108 FT.
NACOOCHEE-HIAWASSEE
ROAD & RECREATION
ASSOCIATION

Twenty-one-year-old Gary Douberly, taking a semester off from the University of Central Florida in Orlando, was five days into his first long-distance hike when he trudged out of the woods at Unicoi Gap (right) in Georgia. Many hikers take a breather in the remarkable old logging town of Helen, Georgia (opposite), which has been transformed into a tidy Alpine village and is jammed with tourists on summer weekends.

By building dams like the 2,365-foot-long, 480-foot-high monolith (above) at Fontana, North Carolina, the Tennessee Valley Authority tamed the wild Little Tennessee River (left) while providing hydroelectric power to parts of seven states. The Appalachian Trail crosses directly over the dam on its way north into the Great Smoky Mountains National Park. Below, thousands of visitors a year fish and boat on Fontana Lake (overleaf).

Rest stops like the Johnny Reb Motel and Crafts Shop on North Carolina Route 28 (top right) abound near the southern Appalachian Trail. Thru hikers remember the "Fontana Hilton" shelter (bottom right) because there are hot showers available at the nearby Tennessee Valley Authority visitor center. Hot Springs, North Carolina, a popular rafting center, offers a unique welcome center of its own (opposite). Sunsets in the Smokies (overleaf) are enrapturing.

YOU ARE ON THE
APPALACHIAN NATIONAL SCENIC TRAIL (A.T.)

MT. KATAHDIN, MAINE
1869 MI.

BIG BALD 48 MI.

LOVERS LEAP 1.5 MI.

SPRINGER MT. GEORGIA
268 MI.

GREAT SMOKY MTNS.
NP 35 MI.

MAX PATCH 15 MI.

ON ITS WILD, MOUNTAIN CREST ROUTE
BETWEEN GEORGIA AND MAINE, THE A.T.
PASSES THROUGH THE TOWN OF HOT
SPRINGS AS IT CROSSES THE FRENCH
BROAD RIVER. HOT SPRINGS IS A
FAVORITE REST STOP OF A.T. HIKERS.
THE A.T. IS MANAGED AND MAINTAINED
HERE BY THE VOLUNTEERS OF THE
CAROLINA MOUNTAIN CLUB, THE
APPALACHIAN TRAIL CONFERENCE, AND
THE USDA FOREST SERVICE.

Whole trail guides have been published describing the array of wildflowers (opposite) that line the Appalachian Trail. "The Grand Floral Parade," Leonard M. Adkins calls it in his visitors' companion. In late May, thickets of rhododendrons (above) blanket entire hillsides in spots like Roan Mountain in Tennessee. Many of the summer flowers, writes Adkins, "continue to bloom long after Cub Scouts have left the woods and have begun thinking about Halloween."

Early birds who left Georgia while trees were just budding will reach the Tennessee Smokies in time to catch the full thrall of spring (above). At Carver's Gap, 5,512 feet up Roan Mountain in the Pigsah-Cherokee National Forest, thru hikers get one of their first clear vistas of sweeping valleys (right). Protecting the mountaintops on the Tennessee–North Carolina border from over-development has been a thorny challenge.

Deborah Smith—trail name "Twilight"—of Medway, Massachusetts; Scott "Flow Easy" Davis of Charlotte, North Carolina; and Scott's trusty trail companion Linville pause along the road in Damascus, Virginia (opposite). All three completed the thru hike—though Linville had to be boarded in two stretches where dogs are not allowed on the trail. Out of Damascus, the trail heads back up the mountains (right) to Feathercamp Ridge.

Hikers in Damascus, Virginia, walk right past the tempting Country Gifts & Antique shop (opposite). Like many Appalachian Trail water crossings, the Little Wolf Creek footbridge (top left) near Bastian, Virginia, was carefully built by hand. In Pearisburg, Virginia, the trail slices between an ordinary house and a grove of trees (bottom left) before heading up Angels Rest Mountain. Deep valleys lie far below the trail in Jefferson National Forest (overleaf).

Virginia A.T. hikers encounter the Audie Murphy Monument (right). Murphy, who was awarded more valorous medals—including three Purple Hearts—than any other U.S. soldier in World War II, became an actor in war movies. He died in 1971 when the plane in which he was traveling crashed near here on Brush Mountain. Hikers must negotiate the "Dragon's Tooth" escarpment (opposite), which looms high above Virginia Route 624.

Here at Virginia's Blackhorse Gap (left) and elsewhere, the Appalachian Trail crosses the scenic Blue Ridge Parkway automobile road through central Virginia. Dave and Chris Wilcox of Newport News, Virginia, are striking figures against the midday sun (above) near Virginia's Humpback Rocks. Both are professional cartographers, veteran hikers, and volunteer trail maintainers for the Old Dominion Appalachian Trail Club.

Without dedicated volunteer trail maintainers, the Appalachian Trail would soon succumb to washouts, overgrowth, and decay. Fran Leckie (above)—here freshening white trail blazes—heads maintenance efforts of Virginia's Old Dominion Trail Club. Club members Floyd Thompson, Dave Wilcox, and David Monahan, left to right, move a small boulder into place (right) to curb erosion. Thompson is a computer programmer, Wilcox a cartographer, and Monahan a claims adjuster.

Hikers like Janet "Interplanet Janet" Offermann (above) of Glen Allen, Virginia, treasure "mail drops" at post offices such as this in Waynesboro, Virginia. Pay phones, too, are a welcome sight. Jim "Field-hand" Schroering of Montpelier, Virginia, rings home (right) outside the Howard Johnson's restaurant, a stone's throw from the trail at Rockfish Gap, Virginia. The thru hiker's backpack (opposite) is loaded with forty pounds of provisions, from a compass to extra underwear.

Bearfence Hut
(opposite), near
Shenandoah National
Park's Skyline Drive,
is a typical crude
A.T. lean-to shelter.
It offers a bunk bed
board on which to
spread sleeping bags,
a simple journal,
and a "bear pole"
(left) on which to
hang food. Not far
away, the trail flattens
at Big Meadows
(overleaf) where A.T.
hikers can easily get
lost amid a labyrinth
of crossing side trails.

One of the boiling controversies in Appalachian Trail history involved the decision in 1935 not to fight construction of the Skyline Drive auto road on the very route of the trail through Shenandoah National Park. The footpath was relocated nearby. Hikers and drivers alike now enjoy spectacular views from overlooks at Indian Run (left) and elsewhere. Above the park, the trail crosses a ridge (above) in northern Virginia's Sky Meadows State Park.

Appalachian Trail hikers must climb not only steep grades but also an occasional barbed-wire or split-log fence (above). Here near Linden, Virginia, and in Pennsylvania—where grazing is still permitted on A.T. property— simple ladders have been built to preserve the fences and give hikers a boost. Above Fiery Run Road in northern Virginia, northbound hikers (right) cross a meadow and head back into the hills.

Hikers near Bluemont, Virginia, can get a respite from the trail at the A.T.C.-owned Bears Den Hostel (above), a twenty-six-bed facility that offers an equipped kitchen, dining room, clean linens and laundry facility, and hostel store—all magic words to a thru hiker's ears. Down a short side trail, Bears Den Rocks (opposite) afford a quiet picnic spot and view of Snickers Gap. This is Potomac Appalachian Trail Club territory.

Historic Harpers Ferry (opposite) is the A.T. thru hiker's psychological mid-point. The Appalachian Trail Conference is headquartered in this tiny town where abolitionist John Brown raided an armory (and was hanged for it) before the Civil War. In town, the trail climbs stone steps (right) carved in the 1920s. It crosses the Potomac River over a pedestrian bridge (overleaf) cantilevered to an old railroad bridge.

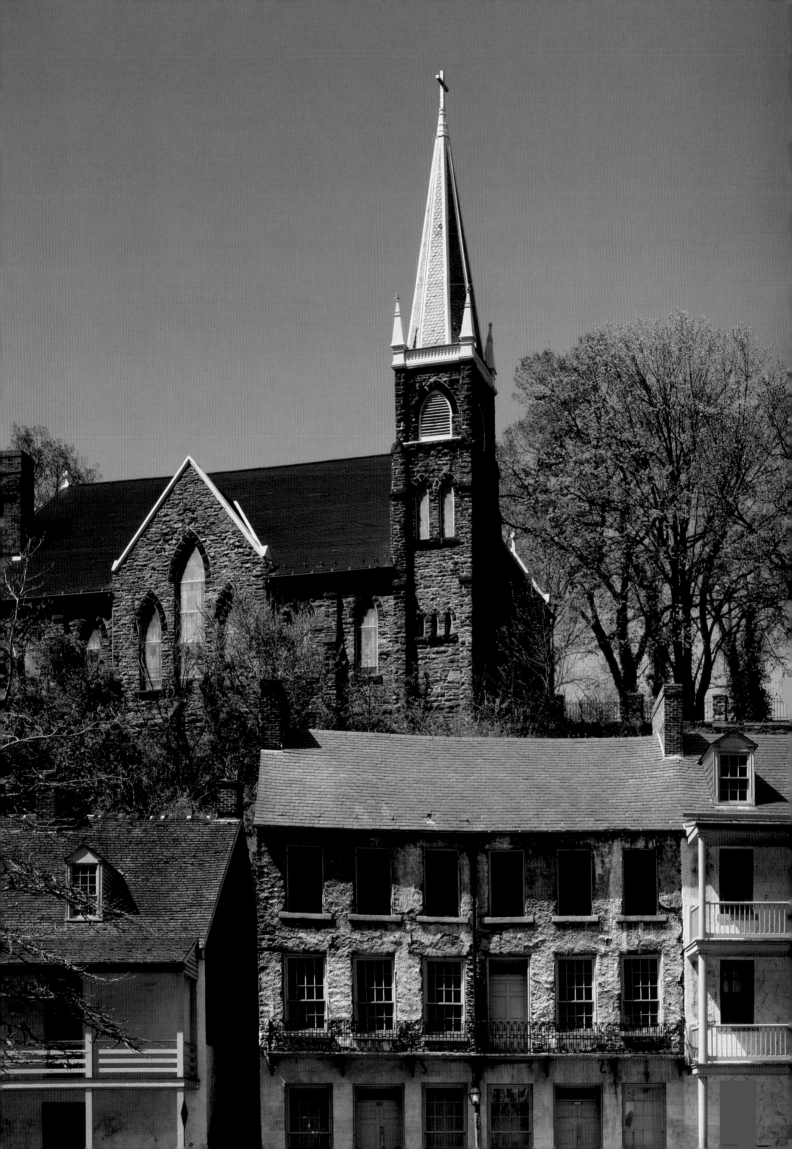

In Maryland, the
Appalachian Trail
passes the remarkable
1896 War Correspon-
dents' Memorial Arch
(opposite). Poet and
novelist George Alfred
Townsend—himself a
Civil War correspon-
dent—designed this
unusual monument to
other war reporters
"whose toils . . .
educated provinces of
rustics into a bright
nation of readers."
The trail also winds
past Maryland's
Washington Monu-
ment (left), unveiled
on Independence
Day 1827 as the
first monument to
the first president of
the United States.

The Appalachian Trail is protected over busy Interstate 70 (top right) near Hagerstown, Maryland. The crossing of Pennsylvania Route 233 near South Mountain (bottom right) is much more rustic. More serene still is this pond in Pennsylvania's Caledonia State Park (opposite). On the edge of the park, the trail passes the Thaddeus Stevens Museum in an old blacksmith shop (overleaf). U.S. Congressman Stevens was a Civil War–era Radical Republican leader of the House of Representatives.

Autumnal splendor envelopes Pennsylvania's Pine Grove Furnace State Park (left), the true midpoint of the Appalachian Trail. If hikers reach it before the park's general store closes for the winter, it's a tradition that they mark the occasion by gorging themselves on a hefty container of ice cream—thus gaining membership in the informal "Half Gallon Club." Back on the trail, they'll pass several cabins and hunting lodges (opposite).

Propped on the porch of the Appalachian Trail Conference's regional headquarters (above) in Boiling Springs, Pennsylvania, is a "swapbox" into which hikers are invited to exchange items like salt, peanut butter, pancake mix, and dried peas. Citizens renamed Boiling Springs Lake (right), which the A.T. skirts, the "Children's Lake" because children from throughout the region crowd the picnic areas and delight in feeding the lake's geese and ducks.

Jim Hewins (right), a steel company sales representative from Levittown, Pennsylvania, and Madison, his half-Labrador retriever, half-Saint Bernard, follow the Appalachian Trail over the Inter-County Bridge outside Duncannon, Pennsylvania. Another dog, Rookie, hiked one thousand miles of the trail in 1987 when Hewins—trail name "Cookie Monster"— completed the entire trail. The Inter-County bridge spans the Juniata River (opposite). The trail then crosses the larger Susquehanna River.

Though down on its luck in recent years, the Hotel Doyle (left) in Duncannon, Pennsylvania, provides hikers a welcome, inexpensive stop. In Port Clinton, Pennsylvania, many hikers eschew hostelries and spread their sleeping bags under the town pavilion (above). Thru hikers pinpoint small towns in their Appalachian Trail Data Books, but in Pennsylvania the most talked-about landmark is the "Pinnacle" formation of treacherous loose rocks (overleaf) north of Port Clinton.

The Appalachian Trail follows the Buttermilk Falls Trail (above) in New Jersey, en route to Rattlesnake Mountain. Even in moderately hilly states, A.T. planners seek high ground. In New Jersey, none is higher than the state park near Sussex that passes the 220-foot High Point Monument (right). The 1930 "monument to New Jersey heroes" offers glorious views of Lake Marcia, the Pocono and Catskills mountains, and Wallkill River Valley.

On a clear day atop Bear Mountain in New York's upper Hudson River Valley, hikers can see Manhattan's distant skyscrapers. The trail below crosses the 1924 Bear Mountain Bridge (opposite) over the Hudson. Nearby, the A.T. runs through the Bear Mountain Zoo where a quick visit usually counts among thru hikers' favorite memories. This bald eagle (above) is kept in captivity because of a broken wing; it could not survive in the wild.

In New York's Harriman State Park, hikers pass beautiful lakes like 320-acre Tiorati (left) and through part of what is often called the trail's "long tunnel of green"—which of course turns spectacularly yellow, orange, and red come fall. At Graymoor Monastery (above), which is right on the trail near Garrison, New York, Franciscan friars and Sisters of the Atonement warmly greet and feed thru hikers and offer welcome shower facilities.

The New York–
New Jersey Trail
Conference—one
of the biggest of A.T.
clubs—has placed a
sturdy trail marker
(above) along New
York Route 22 near
Pawling. Outside
Pawling, the trail
skims the corner of
a farmer's meadow
near this 1957
barn (right). Near
Cornwall Bridge,
Connecticut, the A.T.
drops down to the
Housatonic River,
where hikers share the
outdoors with trout
fishermen like Keith
Ritchie (overleaf).

Not just trees and signposts get a white Appalachian Trail blaze; note the swatch on the Blue Bridge (above) over the Housatonic River near Falls Village, Connecticut. From Jug End Road outside Sheffield, Massachusetts, hikers view Berkshire Mountain ridges they will soon be—or have just finished—surmounting (right). The trail worms past summer cottages along Massachusetts' Goose Pond (overleaf), where there is an ongoing program to move it up the hillside, away from civilization.

A.T. hikers traverse
Mount Greylock
(above), which at
3,491 feet is the highest
peak in Massachu-
setts. A war memorial
on the summit pro-
vides an incomparable
viewpoint overlooking
the surrounding Berk-
shires. Twenty-year-
old Drew Ryan (right)
of North Providence,
Rhode Island, emerges
from the Massachu-
setts woods, heading
to Georgia on an
ambitious "yo-yo"
of the Appalachian
Trail. That means he
completed an entire
thru hike and was
attempting an imme-
diate return trip.

The A.T. crosses the 1977 William D. MacArthur memorial foot-bridge (opposite) near Wallingford, Vermont, as it briefly coincides with the Long Trail in Green Mountain National Forest. Thru hikers in the Green Mountains see some birches (left) and will pass even more in Robert Frost country— the White Mountains of neighboring New Hampshire. The Greens, including Mount Tabor (overleaf), are a far gentler climb than the granite Whites.

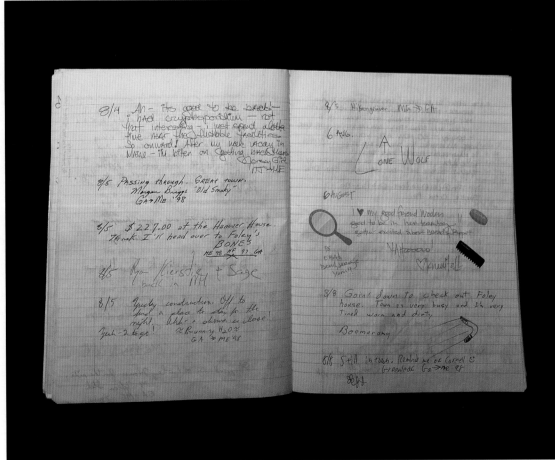

Zion Episcopal Church (opposite) in Manchester Center, Vermont, operates a hostel open to Appalachian Trail hikers. The Inn at Long Trail (top left) in Killington, Vermont, is a favorite A.T. stop. Originally built as a hikers' lodge—see page 16— the rustic chalet is an informal mail drop. The Dartmouth Outing Club maintains a thru-hikers' register (bottom left) at the university's Robinson Hall in Hanover, New Hampshire.

The Appalachian Trail passes through one of New Hampshire's flinty defiles called a "notch." It is at Franconia Notch (left) where one of the state's natural symbols— "The Old Man in the Mountains" (above)—towers above. A.T. hikers are not alone in scaling fierce Mount Washington—the windiest place on earth. Just before they challenge the mountain, many hikers rest at the Lakes of the Cloud Hut. A historic steam-powered cog railway (overleaf) clatters near the trail.

Hikers on Mount
Washington behold
the magnificent 1902
Mount Washington
Hotel and Resort
(above), site of the
1945 Bretton Woods
Economic Confer-
ence. The Presidential
Range (right), where
Mount Washington is
the highest peak, is
not off-limits to
winter hiking, but
conditions are so
unpredictable that it
is best left to skiers
and moose. About
one hundred miles
into Maine, the A.T.
passes along the
Bigelow Range
(overleaf) above the
Carabasset Valley.

The trail is full of ordinary wooden markers, but this one (left) north of Monson carries an ominous warning: "Hikers are about to enter the dreaded 'Wilderness.'" This area is usually snow-covered by early October, and hikers will be unable to resupply for many days. That is all the more reason Monson's "Pie Lady," Sydney Pratt, gets a lot of hiker customers. She also puts up hikers before or after their Wilderness ordeals.

Just as Dahlonega, Georgia, is the acknowledged supply and transportation center at the southern end of the trail, Millinocket, Maine, has become the locus of trail activity at the northern end. There, the 1902 Appalachian Trail Lodge (above) is reputed to have the "best shower," which is certainly most welcome after a twenty-one hundred-mile hike. In town at the Appalachian Trail Café (opposite), emaciated thru hikers often eat two or three meals at a sitting.

For northbound hikers, the Abol Bridge (opposite) over the Penobscot River marks the end of the terrible Wilderness and a place for easy striding before the last push up Mount Katahdin. In Baxter State Park, all hikers are warned of fire danger (above) and reminded that pets are not allowed. A moose bog (overleaf) is beautiful much of the year but come mid-October, Mount Katahdin is off-limits to thru-hikers and campers and is only open to people who are day hiking.

Locals painted a boulder (top right) to welcome hikers and other visitors to Baxter State Park. A Katahdin Stream Campground sign (bottom right) gives southbounders daunting news: They have more than two thousand miles to go to Georgia. "We made it!" photos (opposite) are de rigueur atop Mount Katahdin. It is clear why Abenaki Indians called Maine's highest mountain (overleaf)—now the northern terminus of the Appalachian Trail—Katahdin, which means "greatest mountain."

"Willow"
GA → ME 97

KATAHDIN
APPALACHIAN TRAIL

& Pokey   GA-ME '96

Index

Page numbers in italics refer to illustrations.

Abol Bridge, 10, 21, *121*
Amicalola Falls and State Park, *4, 11*
Appalachian Mountain Club, 7
Appalachian Trail Café and A.T. Lodge, 14, *118*
Appalachian Trail Conference, 7, *7*, 8, 11, 12–13, 19, 20, 66, 78, 128

Patches with the famous A.T. symbol are available to all hikers. Those completing two thousand or more miles may add that coveted designation. The person who would wear this patch is also a volunteer trail maintainer and an Appalachian Trail Conference member. The A.T.C. makes other distinctive patches available as well.

Appalachian Trail monogram, patches, plaques, 8, *12*, 22, *92*, *128*
Avery, Myron H., 8, *14*, *15*, 20

Backpack contents, 9, *54*
Bastian, Virginia, *45*
Baxter State Park, 8, 10, *121*, 124
Bear Mountain Bridge and Zoo, *15*, 89
Bearfence Hut, *57*
Bears Den Hostel and Rocks, 18, *65*
Big Meadows, *57*
Bigelow Range, *112*
Blackhorse Gap, *51*
Blazes, 17–18, *52*, *96*
Blue Bridge, *96*
Blue Ridge Parkway, *8*, 51
Bluemont, Virginia, *65*
Boiling Springs, Pennsylvania, *78*
Bretton Woods, New Hampshire, 20, *112*
Bryson, Bill, 9–10, *15*, 21

Clingmans Dome, 7
Cogswell, Don, 8

Commercialization, 12
Connecticut portion, 18, *92*, *96*
Cornwall Bridge, *92*

Dahlonega, Georgia, 19, *118*
Damascus, Virginia, 20, *42*, 45
Dartmouth Outing Club, 107
Davis, Scott, *42*
Dotter, Kyra, 13–14
Douberly, Gary, *28*
Dragon's Tooth, *48*
Duncannon, Pennsylvania, *80*, 83

Erwin, Tennessee, 19–20

Falls Village, Connecticut, *96*
Field, David B., 21
Flip-flopping, 19
Fontana Dam and Lake, *31*
"Fontana Hilton," *34*
Franconia Notch, *109*

Gatewood, Emma "Grandma," 20
Georgia Appalachian Trail Club, *4*
Georgia portion, 4, 8, 11, 16, 22, *26*, *28*
Goad, Phil, 19
Goose Pond, *96*
Graymoor Monastery, *91*
Great Smoky Mountains National Park, 10, 20, *31*, *34*, 40
Green Mountains, *103*
Greene, Walter, 11

"Half Gallon Club," *77*
Hall, Warner, 12
Hanover, New Hampshire, 9, *107*
Harriman State Park, *91*
Harpers Ferry, West Virginia, 7, 12, 13, 20, 66
Helen, Georgia, 19, *28*
Hewins, Jim, *80*
High Point Monument, *86*
Horton, David, 10
Hot Springs, North Carolina, *34*

International Appalachian Trail, 21
Irwin, Bill, 10

Johnny Reb Motel and Crafts Shop, *34*
Journals and registers, trail, 19, *107*
Jug End Road, *96*

Killington, Vermont, *107*
King, Brian, 9

Lake Marcia, *86*
Lake Tiorati, *91*
Leckie, Fran, 17, 18, 19, *52*
Lexington, Virginia, 20
Linden, Virginia, *62*
Long Trail, *13*, *103*
Long Trail, Inn at, *16*, *107*

MacArthur, William D., Footbridge, *103*
MacKaye, Benton, 7, *9*, 18, 20
Maine portion, *4*, 7, 8, 10, *14*, *15*, *112*, *117*, *118*, *121*, 124
Maintainers, trail, 17–19, *52*
Manchester Center, Vermont, *107*
Maryland portion, 17, 71, 72
Massachusetts portion, *96*, 100
Millinocket, Maine, 8, 14, *118*
Monahan, David, *52*
Monson, Maine, 10, *117*
Mount Greylock, 100
Mount Katahdin, 4, 8, 10, *14*, *15*, 21, *121*, 124
Mount Tabor, *103*
Mount Washington and Presidential Range, 7, 10, *109*, *112*
Mount Washington Hotel and cog railway, *109*, *112*
"Murderous Mary," 19–20
Murphy, Audie, Monument, *48*

National Park Service, 12, 20, 21
Neels Gap, 22
New Hampshire portion, 7, 10, *107*, *109*, *112*
New Jersey portion, 18, *86*
New York portion, 7–8, *15*, *89*, *91*, *92*
New York–New Jersey Trail Conference, *92*
Newell, "Buddy" and Randy, 15–17
North Carolina portion, 7, *31*, *34*, 40
Nuckolls, Steve, 19

Offermann, Janet, 14–15, *54*
Old Dominion Appalachian Trail Club, 17, 18, *51*, *52*
Old Man in the Mountains, *109*
Overuse of trail, 20–21

Palisades International Park, 7–8
Palmerton, Pennsylvania, *4*
Pawling, New York, *92*
Pearisburg, Virginia, *45*
Pennsylvania portion, *4*, *72*, *77*, 78, *80*, 83

Pie Lady of Monson, Maine, *117*
Pine Grove Furnace, Pennsylvania, 20, *77*
Pinnacle, The, *83*
Port Clinton, Pennsylvania, *83*
Potomac Appalachian Trail Club, 65

Relocation off roads, 18, *21*, 61
Ritchie, Keith, *96*
Roan Mountain, 40
Ryan, Drew, *100*

Sands, Mary, 7
Schroering, Jim, *54*
Shaffer, Earl, 8, *18*, 19
Shelters and hostels, 18, 19, *34*, *57*, 65
Shenandoah National Park, *57*, 61
Sky Meadows State Park, 61
Skyline Drive, 19, *57*, 61
Smith, Deborah, *42*
Smoky Mountains (*see* Great Smoky Mountains National Park)
Snickers Gap, 65
Speed record, 10
Springer Mountain, 4, 8, 11, 16, 22
Stevens, Thaddeus, Museum, *72*

Tennessee portion, *39*, 40
Thompson, Floyd, *52*
Tidewater Appalachian Trail Club, 12
Townsend, George Alfred, 71
Trail names, 8–9, 19

Unicoi Gap, *4*, 28

Vermont portion, 7, 10, *103*, *107*
Virginia portion, 10, 12, 17, 18, 19, *42*, *45*, *48*, *51*, *52*, *54*, *57*, 61, *62*, 65

Walasi Yi Center, *26*
War Correspondents' Memorial Arch, 71
Washington Monument (Maryland), *71*
White Mountains, *103* (*see* also Mount Washington)
Wilcox, Dave and Chris, *51*, 52
Wilderness, Hundred-Mile, 10, *117*
Woodstock, Vermont, 20

Yo-yoing, 19, *100*

Zion Episcopal Church, *107*